Read what others have said about
Dani Johnson's Prospecting and Closing
Script Book™ *Supplemental*

"After getting Dani's Script Book I increased my productivity using cold leads. I decreased the time I worked my business. I MORE than doubled my income. I don't even pick up the phone if a prospect calls unless I have Dani's scripts in front of me!"

~ Jackie O'Quinn

"The Script Book has done a lot for my business in so far as it taught me to LISTEN to the prospect and to fish with their worm, not my cheesecake. As I used it more and more it gave me posture because I was confident about what to say next and where I was leading the prospect. I have improved my sign-up rate tremendously using the Script Book."

~ Michele Castle

"Your Script Book is great and has inspired my dynamic daughter to join my business!"

~ Deborah Cameron

"I am so excited about Dani's Script Book and CD's! They have already changed my outlook on this business, the way I handle my calls, and even the way I handle my day to day interactions with people I know and love. The script has given me a confidence I didn't know I had in me!"

~ *Felicity Sevanick*

"Dani's scripts are simple and straightforward!"

~ *Mary Jane Brockman*

"I have loved your Script Book and it really helped me be better on the phone with cold contacts."

~ *Debbie Younkin*

"Well, after 2 weeks of listening to your online calls and using your Script Book, my consultant did over $70,000 in volume. IN JUST 2 WEEKS!!!"

~ *Kathe Ray*

"As a result of First Steps To Success and also listening to your Script Book CD's I was able to sponsor one person shortly before I went to First Steps To Success and one immediately after. Then I sponsored another two..."

~ *Jonathan Kawamura*

"I've been using the scripts and ideas from your script training CD's and have found them to be great. I now really enjoy meeting new people and just chatting with them, getting to know them better. I find I am more relaxed so I don't come across as selling, and am enrolling more high profile people to my team than I was able to before. I am sharing what I know with my team and sending them to your website too."

~ Barb Underdown

"I have recently purchased your Script Book. My confidence in doing the business has soared and my networking is becoming more professional and more 'bigger-picture' focused. Thank you for an awesome resource."

~ Nerissa Bentley

"The Script Book has been fantastic for me, helping me 'heaps' to improve my business and the way I approach people. My business has doubled in a very short time."

~ Inanna Lawton

"To say the least, power is in your Script Book. KNOWLEDGE and POWER together are what I believe I have gained by reading your literature and listening to your CD's.

~ Robert Henry

3

"I am in the process of going through it (the Script Book) a second time, and then a third time. I love it so far!

~ *Joe Rotondo*

"I had purchased your North Carolina CD's and your Script Book about a month ago and I have listened to them - START TO FINISH - 4 times! YOU have turned the light on for me!"

~ *Debbie Scalise*

"After purchasing your Script Book and listening to your on-line training I began to see immediate results. From now on, everyone I sponsor must tap into your training!"

~ *Carolyn Hickerson*

"I am going to have to get another Script Book as mine is so worn, it is ready to fall apart. I am telling all of my new brokers that your Script Book is a 'must'!"

~ *Kathleen Bard*

"I love the Script Book – it keeps me on track and focused. It's easy and simple."

~ *Janina Bitz-Vasquez*

4

"The posture I learned in your Script Book has helped me to show others the type of posture to have."

~ *Sal Puma*

"I am so happy I bought the Script Book. I have been listening everyday to the CD's for a few weeks!"

~ *Brenda Abraham*

"The Script Book has helped me build up more confidence with my client customer base. It has helped me come from a position of power and posture dialog with people on a real, simple level."

~ *Steven Underwood*

"The Script Book has helped me to be better at talking to prospects on the phone."

~ *Wendi*

"The Script Book is so great. I would always try to remember what some of the successful people said, and here it is in a book!"

~ *Dee Platt*

5

"I am a new subscriber and was really excited to get the Script Book. It has been tremendous in getting me past that initial call with the prospect."

~ Kim Redd

"After purchasing the Script Book and attending the Gold Coast First Steps to Success Seminar I wanted to tell everyone in my company about this AWESOME RESOURCE."

~ Tracy

"I am new at using scripts and I love this little book of Gold. It has given me the confidence to talk to leads and be successful in delivery of information they need to hear."

~ Catherine Adams

"I just wanted Dani to know that I'm using her scripts exclusively and setting appointments daily. Thanks, Dani keep up the good information. I love your stuff!"

~ Sue Kyer

"Once I actually started using the Script Book 'word-for-word' and didn't change anything, my ratio went from 1 out of 10 to 5 out of 10!"

~ Charla Hall (Ellie)

"For 11 months I groveled through leads trying to 'convert' the inconvertible. Then when a REAL prospect came along, I had no idea what to do! I NEVER ENROLLED A SINGLE COLD LEAD! After plugging into Dani's training and 2 CD set I closed 2 out of 14 leads, then plugged them into Dani's training so they too could start their path to success."

~ Kris Wood

"The Script Book is GREAT! It makes it so simple to pick up the phone and share my opportunity!"

~ Robyn Leatherbury

"You have been very inspirational to me. I bought your Script Book and have really enjoyed it."

~ Susan Dollinger

"My whole idea of how to do cold calling from a lead list is forever changed. I can't believe that I have been listening to 'experts' tell me how to do it and all I ever got was a stomach ache! Your way of teaching through the scripts makes me feel so natural when I'm calling people now."

~ Margie Jauch

"I appreciated the Script Book because it takes the dread out of making calls and gives me the words to say."

~ Christina Carlton

7

Dani Johnson's Prospecting & Closing
Script Book™
Supplemental

Dani Johnson's
Prospecting and Closing Script Book™ *Supplemental*

ISBN: 0-9789551-1-0

Printed in the United States of America

TABLE OF CONTENTS

More Dani Johnson Closing Scripts

Some Helpful Tips

• The idea of these scripts is not for you to be doing the "selling". It is for you to be interviewing and sorting for the serious prospects.

• Use a process other than yourself to "present" the details of your company, opportunity or product. For example, use a web site, recorded call, live call, audio or video tape (CD or DVD), live meeting, or even a 3-way call with your sponsor/ upline.

• Work as many leads and talk to as many prospects monthly as possible. It often takes up to 90 days to fill your "pipeline" and start really seeing big results. Once you build momentum, it will get easier and easier and your profits will multiply. Commit to a marketing plan and stick with it. If you are working leads, work them consistently!

• Practice the scripts on friends and family or other business associates. Many people have had success by simply asking a friend if they could "practice" a new script on them that they were learning. The friend ends up saying, "Hey that sounds interesting. Can I do it too?" Or... "Can I get more information about that?"

• Learn Dani Johnson's Core Rapport Methodology™ and the F.O.R.M. acronym to ask questions and instantly build trust with your prospects. You will discover their needs, strengths and goals during the Initial Contact phase with the scripts. Take notes and refer back to their needs, strengths and goals when closing and handling objections. F.O.R.M. stands for Family, Occupation, Recreation and Message.

While it is very simple, it is a VERY powerful technique when used correctly along with other Dani Johnson Core Rapport Methodology™ principles.

• Use a follow-up system (personal call, thank you note, postcard, email auto responder, etc.). Statistics show you will increase your ratios significantly by following up with good prospects.

• Realize that leaders continue to do the key activities that make them money (selling product and signing up new reps) even when they don't "feel" like it. So learn how to consistently make yourself do the things you do not want to do.

• Think long term. It may take some time to find your flow and get the results you desire. Set goals. Reinvest back into your business monthly – into your advertising and lead generation programs and most importantly into your education, training and motivation.

• Use the Appendix pages at the back of this book. If you are looking for quality leads for your business, see our recommended vendors list available to all registered FREE members at DaniJohnson.com.

More Dani Johnson
Prospecting Scripts

Friend Blown Out Of The Water

Script Tip!
SMILE WHILE YOU'RE ON THE PHONE. YOU ARE NOT A SALESPERSON, YOU ARE A BUSINESS DEVELOPER.

F.O.R.M. your warm contacts. Remember you are the interviewer.

Hi **"PROSPECT'S NAME"**, how's it going?
I'm calling to make things right with you and to ask you for forgiveness. I feel really bad about the way I approached you concerning a business. I didn't take into consideration your feelings. I was self-centered and I had my own agenda at hand. I feel like I put a damper on our relationship and by giving you an incomplete picture about what's going on you made up your mind on misinformation and I don't want you coming back to me a year from now saying "Hey, how come you didn't let me in on this?"

So **"PROSPECT'S NAME"**, *(pause)* you are not coming off my list until you take a look. And if you take a look at the whole picture and you say it's not for you I promise you I will not bug you again about it. Who knows it may be a way that you can *(repeat their needs, strengths and goals)*. So when's a good time for us to get together?

People You Haven't Talked To In Years

> ### Script Tip!
> *SMILE WHILE YOU'RE ON THE PHONE. YOU ARE NOT A SALESPERSON, YOU ARE A BUSINESS DEVELOPER.*
>
> *F.O.R.M. your warm contacts. Remember you are the interviewer.*

Hi **"PROSPECT'S NAME"**, how's it going? This is **"YOUR NAME"**. You know I was thinking about you the other day and I wrote your name down to give you a call. How are you? What have you been up to? *(F.O.R.M. your warm contacts. Find their needs, strengths and goals.)*

Hey **"PROSPECT'S NAME"**, you know you mentioned *(repeat what their need was)*. I work with a company that is expanding all over the country right now. I don't know if you have the skills and qualities of the kind of person that they're looking for and I'm sure you're totally satisfied with your current job, but let's exchange phone numbers. I can get you the information of what they have available and then we can go from there. If it's a match, great. If not, that's fine too. At least it's a chance for you to *(repeat their need)*. So when are you available?

Well that depends of course on the kind of qualities and skills that you have and at this point we really don't know what that is. It's at least a chance to *(repeat their need)*. If it works for you, great, if not, that's fine too. So when are you available?

People You Are Terrified To Talk To

> ### Script Tip!
> *SMILE WHILE YOU'RE ON THE PHONE. YOU ARE NOT A SALESPERSON, YOU ARE A BUSINESS DEVELOPER.*
>
> *F.O.R.M. your warm contacts. Remember you are the interviewer.*

Hi **"PROSPECT'S NAME"**, how's it going? This is **"YOUR NAME"**. I am terrified to be calling you right now *(pause)* because I really respect who you are and you are very intelligent and I hope to someday be successful as you. And I really don't know how you feel about me but I really want to be able to do the kind of things that you are doing. I really would appreciate your assessment on something that I am looking at. Is there anyway that we can meet?

Great! What is your schedule like tomorrow?
I have **"DAY & TIME"** or **"DAY & TIME"** open.
Which is best for you?

After Leaving A Training Seminar

> ***Script Tip!***
> *SMILE WHILE YOU'RE ON THE PHONE. YOU ARE NOT A SALESPERSON, YOU ARE A BUSINESS DEVELOPER.*
>
> *F.O.R.M. your warm contacts. Remember you are the interviewer.*

Hi, **"PROSPECT'S NAME"**, how's it going? This is **"YOUR NAME"**. I've just come out of a training seminar and I really need some practice on some people. And I need to practice on some people that I know love me and can give me an honest assessment about what I am doing. Would you be willing to let me practice on you so that I don't blow it with a bunch of other people?

Great! What is your schedule like tomorrow?
I have **"DAY & TIME"** or **"DAY & TIME"** open.
Which is best for you?

Additional Warm Market Script #1

> ***Script Tip!***
> *SMILE WHILE YOU'RE ON THE PHONE. YOU ARE NOT A SALESPERSON, YOU ARE A BUSINESS DEVELOPER.*
>
> *F.O.R.M. your warm contacts. Remember you are the interviewer.*

Hi **"PROSPECT'S NAME"**, how's it going?
Hey **"PROSPECT'S NAME"**, I was talking to a friend of mine who works high up in a large corporation and "he/she" has some positions available with "his/her" company. "He/she" was asking me if I knew of anyone who possesses a good attitude and personal skills and I immediately thought of you. I don't know if it will work out for you or not but you might know of someone who is looking for full-time or part-time work.

Because of their success rate with personal referrals, they prefer to offer this to people who come highly recommended before those from newspaper advertisements. I know you are probably happy with what you're currently doing, but part-time people with the company are earning about $2000-$3000 a month. They also have full-time options available.

Because of "his/her" position in the corporation it is extremely hard to talk with "him/her." I can get you an introduction to **"SPONSOR'S NAME"** and "he/she" can tell you more about what's available. If the two of you decide you like each other you can go from there. When are you available?

(Edify your sponsor/expert)

IF THEY BEGIN ASKING A LOT OF QUESTIONS:

I really don't know all of the facts and I don't want to confuse you. The best thing is for you to meet with **"SPONSOR'S NAME"**. Just check it out and if it works out for you great, if not that's fine too. At least it is a way for you to check out another option. So when are you available?

CREATE URGENCY AND EXCITEMENT!!!

Additional Warm Market Script #2

> ***Script Tip!***
> *SMILE WHILE YOU'RE ON THE PHONE. YOU ARE NOT A SALESPERSON, YOU ARE A BUSINESS DEVELOPER.*
>
> *F.O.R.M. your warm contacts. Remember you are the interviewer.*

Hi **"PROSPECT'S NAME"**, how's it going?

Look **"PROSPECT'S NAME"**, I've stumbled across something that can help you *(repeat their needs, strengths and goals)*. It's probably not for you, but if you are as serious about *(repeat their needs)*, do you feel it would be worth your time to get together so you can see how you could *(repeat their needs, strengths and goals)*?

Great! What is your schedule like tomorrow?

I have **"DAY & TIME"** or **"DAY & TIME"** open.

Which is best for you?

Warm Contact Referral Script #1

> **Script Tip!**
> *SMILE WHILE YOU'RE ON THE PHONE. YOU ARE NOT
> A SALESPERSON, YOU ARE A BUSINESS DEVELOPER.*
>
> *F.O.R.M. your warm contacts. Remember you are
> the interviewer.*
>
> *Remeber to edify your associate/expert and that you are
> the interviewer.*

Hi **"PROSPECT'S NAME"**, how's it going? This is
"YOUR NAME". Your name came up in conversation
several times when I was talking with a friend of yours, **"AS-
SOCIATE'S NAME".** How do you know **"ASSOCIATE'S
NAME"**? *(F.O.R.M. your warm contact. Find their needs,
strengths and goals.)*

When I asked **"ASSOCIATE'S NAME"** if "he/she" knew
of anyone who possessed a good attitude and personal skills,
your name came up. So do you feel you have a good attitude
and personal skills?

Well because of our success rate with personal references, we
would prefer to offer positions to people who come highly
recommended before those from newspaper advertisements.
You may be totally happy with what you're currently doing,
but we are targeting the **"CITY/STATE"** area because of
growth that we are experiencing and we need help.

We are looking for a few Coordinators who can work well with and manage people and someone who can learn a company training program and communicate it effectively to others. Do you feel that you could do that? The income of a Coordinator just starting out is $_____.

Is that what you would be looking for? This may or may not work out for you but at least it is a way for you to *(repeat their needs, strengths and goals)*.

So I would love to meet you in person and share for about 45 minutes so you can get a better understanding of our company and training program. At that time I will also explain the growth we are experiencing in this area and the type of income you could expect to earn your first year. Then if it's a match we can go from there. When are you available?

CREATE URGENCY AND EXCITEMENT!!!!!

Warm Contact Referral Script #2

Script Tip!
SMILE WHILE YOU'RE ON THE PHONE. YOU ARE NOT A SALESPERSON, YOU ARE A BUSINESS DEVELOPER.

F.O.R.M. your warm contacts. Remember you are the interviewer.

Hi **"PROSPECT'S NAME"**, how's it going? This is **"YOUR NAME"**. **"ASSOCIATE'S NAME"** asked me to give you a call. How do you know **"ASSOCIATE'S NAME"**? *(F.O.R.M. your warm contact. Find their needs, strengths and goals.)*

Hey **"PROSPECT'S NAME"**, you know, you mentioned *(repeat what their need was)*. I happen to work with a company that is expanding all over the country right now and specifically in **"PROSPECT'S LOCAL AREA"**. Now, I don't know if you have the skills and qualities of the kind of person that our company would be looking for, but we are doing a few interviews looking for key people that can head up an entire organization right there in the **"CITY/STATE"** area. I can get you some information of what they have available and we can go from there. If it's a match great. If not, that's fine too. At least it's a chance for you to *(repeat their needs)*.

Do you have a calendar handy? When would be a good time to get together so I can get some information to you to see if maybe you might have the kind of qualities of the kind of person we are looking for?

> ### *Script Tip!*
> *Book the appointment immediately. Don't schedule too far out. There is no urgency in next week.*

> ### *Script Tip!*
> *If they say no or if you don't find their need ask for a referral and use the script below.*

We prefer offering these types of positions to people who come highly recommended to us. So do you know of anyone that might be looking for a leadership role in a very successful corporation?

Warm Market Interview Script

> ### *Script Tip!*
> *SMILE WHILE YOU'RE ON THE PHONE. YOU ARE NOT A SALESPERSON, YOU ARE A BUSINESS DEVELOPER.*
>
> *F.O.R.M. your warm contacts. Remember you are the interviewer.*

Hello **"PROSPECT'S NAME"**, how are you?
"PROSPECT'S NAME", I have a question for you.
(Ask one of the following questions listed below.)

A. How serious are you about making some serious money this month?
B. Are you open for a lucrative change?
C. Do you feel that an extra $5000 a month would improve your current financial situation?
D. How would you like to capitalize on your people skills, contacts, expertise, experience and knowledge?
E. Would you work hard if you had a career option to double your income?

Are you serious about that?
Tell me why?
Great, we need to talk!

Look **"PROSPECT'S NAME"**, I've got something that may or may not work out for you. But I think you should at least take a look at it.

Now **"PROSPECT'S NAME"**, upon receiving the information, you're going to see for yourself whether or not you wish to act on it. I am going to have you listen to *(a brief audio message, conference call, website, 1 on 1, etc.)* to see if you'd like to get more information on how you can *(repeat one of the statements above A, B, C, etc.)* fair enough?

Ok, let's go to *(3-way them to the pre-recorded message, conference call, website, 1 on 1, etc.)*

Edify your sponsor/expert

Your Next Step...

When the call is done go right into question #1 of the **_Follow-Up & Closing Script_** *in Dani Johnson's Prospecting and Closing Script Book™.*

Warm Market Conference Call Script

> ### Script Tip!
> *SMILE WHILE YOU'RE ON THE PHONE. YOU ARE NOT A SALESPERSON, YOU ARE A BUSINESS DEVELOPER.*
>
> *F.O.R.M. your warm contacts. Remember you are the interviewer.*

Hi **"PROSPECT'S NAME"**, how's it going? This is **"YOUR NAME."** There is a new company that is expanding **"NATIONWIDE/INTERNATIONALLY"** and they are opening up the market in your area. They are looking for a couple of key people to work with. I have an in with the company. I can refer you to **"SPONSOR'S NAME"**. *(Build up the sponsor)*

This may or may not work out for you but who knows it might be a way for you to *(repeat their needs, strengths and goals)*. All I know is the company is moving very fast. Do you have a pen and paper handy? Write this phone number down. *(give conference call phone number)* Are you available at _____ or _____? Great I'll call you 5 minutes before, and take you to the call. Okay, I'll talk to you later. Bye.

CREATE URGENCY AND EXCITEMENT!!!

(Edify the speakers or testimonials that are going to be on that call)

Warm Market Client Contact Script

> **INSTRUCTIONS:** *Use the following script if you are in a profession where you see clients everyday (i.e. CPA, Hairdresser, etc). F.O.R.M. your warm contacts.*

Script Tip!
SMILE WHILE YOU'RE ON THE PHONE. YOU ARE NOT A SALESPERSON, YOU ARE A BUSINESS DEVELOPER.

F.O.R.M. your warm contacts. Remember you are the interviewer.

Hey **"PROSPECT'S NAME"**, you know you mentioned *(repeat what their need was)*. I know of a friend that works with a company that is expanding all over the country/world right now. I don't know if you have the skills and qualities of the kind of person that they're looking for and I'm sure you're totally satisfied with your current job. Maybe I can get you some information of what they have available and then we can go from there. If it's a match, great, if not, that's fine too. At least it's a chance for you to *(repeat their need)*.

So when's a good time to call you with the information?

Well that depends of course on the kind of qualities and skills that you have, and at this point we really don't know what that is. It's at least a chance for you to *(repeat their need)*.

If it's a match, great, if not, that's fine too.

So when's a good time to call you?

(Schedule for a web presentation, conference call, 1 on 1 presentation, etc.)

Opt-In Leads

> **INSTRUCTIONS:** *IF the prospect has already seen your website through your advertising and has left their contact information for you to call them and this is your 1st verbal contact with your prospect, use this script.*

> **Script Tip!**
> *SMILE WHILE YOU'RE ON THE PHONE. YOU ARE NOT A SALESPERSON, YOU ARE A BUSINESS DEVELOPER.*
>
> *F.O.R.M. your prospects. Remember you are the interviewer.*

Hi **"PROSPECT'S NAME"**, how's it going? This is **"YOUR NAME"**. You requested some information after reviewing my website at *(www._____.com)* so I'm just giving you a call back. What can I do for you?

Do you have a pen and paper handy? To save us both time, I need to ask you a few questions to figure out what information to direct you to.

Some Questions To Ask Are:
Are you currently working from home? *(if yes)* What is it? *(if no)* What do you do for a living? How long? What do you like about it? What do you dislike about it? Are you thinking of replacing your current income or just supplementing it? Are you married? Do you have kids? Have you ever been self employed or owned a home business before?

Now what level of income are you accustomed to? What kind of income are you looking to generate in the next 12 months? Do you have some capital set aside to start your business?

You know **"PROSPECT'S NAME"**, our company has quite a standard for the people we are looking for. There's a lot of work on our part in setting someone up in a home business successfully. So we are looking for people who are absolutely serious about building a business and making money from home. So **"PROSPECT'S NAME"**, how serious are you about starting a home business? Tell me why?

Great, let me tell you a little bit more about the company I work with.

> **INSTRUCTIONS:** *Your company track record should be 30 - 60 seconds max. Stay away from PRODUCT/SERVICE information.*
>
> *See Appendix B in Dani Johnson's Prospecting and Closing Script Book™.*

Now **"PROSPECT'S NAME"**, the person we're looking for has 3 main qualities; they are a team player, self-motivated and dependable. Do you feel you have these qualities?

Great!
Do you still have a pen and paper handy?
Do you have internet access?
I want to confirm your email address.
What's the best email to contact you at?

FOR A WEB PRESENTATION

I'll be sending you a link to our website to make sure that you get the information. Hey by the way, do you have access to the internet while talking to me? Go ahead and go over to the computer now. I want to make sure that you don't have any problems downloading the information.

Script Tip!
While they are getting to their computer, get them talking about what's important to them. Edify whatever presentation method you use, whether it's a website, live conference call, etc. Always edify your leadership.

Were you able to download the information? Make sure and take really good notes because on this website is the information that you requested so that you can *(repeat their needs, strengths and goals).*
(EDIFY THE WEBSITE)

FOR A LIVE CONFERENCE CALL

The next step is to direct you to a LIVE interactive call where you will get the information you requested so that you can *(repeat their needs, strengths and goals).*

FOR A PRE-RECORDED CALL

The next step is to take you to a brief audio message about our company. This is where you can find the information you requested so that you can *(repeat their needs, strengths and goals).*

FOR A LIVE MEETING or 1 ON 1 PRESENTATION

The next step is for us to meet in person so you can get the rest of the information available so that you will be able to *(repeat their needs, strengths and goals)*.

FOR A FAX MACHINE

Do you have access to a fax machine?
(If yes, fax them the information or give them your FOD# [fax on demand.] You can also get their mailing address to send them an information pack if you want)

Let me give you my phone number: **"YOUR NUMBER"**. We're pre-screening a lot of people right now. We'll be making a decision real soon, so the sooner you can go to *(website, live conference call, pre-recorded call, live meeting, live 1 on 1 presentation, fax machine)* the better. Depending on what your response is to this information will determine whether or not we will work together and where you fit in on our team. If you're available **"DATE & TIME"**, I'll call you back and we'll see if it's a match. So does **"DAY & TIME"** work for you? Ok, talk to you soon.

INSTRUCTIONS: *Set an appointment and follow up with them. If on the web, it needs to be 15 minutes not 2 days. There is no urgency in 2 days. There is urgency in NOW!*

During the follow up, build rapport and start asking these questions:

Hi **"PROSPECT'S NAME"**, how's it going? *(build rapport)* Did you get a chance to review that information yet? Great.

> **Script Tip!**
> *This is a good place to insert your personal testimony. For example: "Prior to getting started...*

1. What did you like about what you saw? *(heard, read, etc.)*

2. Tell me more about that. *(Let them sell themselves. Take notes here, you should already have some notes from your first phone call with them.)*

3. Okay, **"PROSPECT'S NAME"**, do you want to make a little or a lot?

4. What for?

5. **"PROSPECT'S NAME"**, at your current job, how long will it take you to be able to *(list the needs, strengths and goals they just gave you)?*

6. Where do you see yourself getting started, at the bottom working slowly towards *(repeat their needs, strengths and goals)* or do you want to be in a position where you can earn 2 times the amount of money for the same amount of work and effort?

Great! Welcome aboard. How do you want your name spelled on your checks?

Go-Getter Script To Bring Someone To A Live Presentation

> ### Script Tip!
> *SMILE WHILE YOU'RE ON THE PHONE. YOU ARE NOT A SALESPERSON, YOU ARE A BUSINESS DEVELOPER.*
>
> *F.O.R.M. your prospects. Remember you are the interviewer.*

Hi **"PROSPECT'S NAME"**, how's it going? This is **"YOUR NAME"**. There is a company that is expanding **"NATIONWIDE/INTERNATIONALLY"** and they are targeting the **"CITY/STATE"** area. They are currently running an advertising campaign because they're looking for a few key people to head up an entire organization. I have a contact within the company. I can refer you to **"SPONSOR'S NAME"**. *(Edify the sponsor/expert)* Because of their position in the corporation it is extremely hard to get in to see this person.

This may or may not work out for you but this company is moving very fast. They have part-time and full-time options available. Who knows it might be a chance for you to be able to *(repeat their needs, strengths and goals)*. It's definitely worth your time. So when are you available?

> **INSTRUCTIONS:** *IF the prospect begins to ask you a lot of questions, use the script below.*

I really don't know all of the facts and I don't want to confuse you. It obviously depends on your skills and qualifications. The best thing is for you to meet with **"SPONSOR'S NAME"**. Just check it out and if it works out for you great, if not that's fine too. Who knows it might be a way that you can *(repeat their needs, strengths and goals)*. So when are you available?

If the prospect begins to ask you "What is it?", use the script below.

It's a company that is expanding **"NATIONWIDE/INTERNATIONALLY"**. **"SPONSOR'S NAME"** is a highly respected person in the corporation and when you meet with "him/her," "he/she" will be able to answer all of your questions. It may or may not work out for you. Once you meet with **"SPONSOR'S NAME"** you will figure that out. It's definitely worth your time to meet with "him/her." Who knows it might be a way you can *(repeat their needs, strengths and goals)*. So when are you available?

41

DVD Script

> *INSTRUCTIONS: Use this phone script to get your company DVD in someone's hands. Your goal is to get them to watch it immediately and give you names of people they know that this could apply to or who knows it may apply to them. HAVE FUN!*

Script Tip!
SMILE WHILE YOU'RE ON THE PHONE. YOU ARE NOT A SALESPERSON, YOU ARE A BUSINESS DEVELOPER.

F.O.R.M. your prospects. Remember you are the interviewer.

Hi **"PROSPECT'S NAME"**, how's it going? This is **"YOUR NAME"**. There is an established corporation that is expanding **"NATIONWIDE/INTERNATIONALLY"**. They are specifically targeting **"CITY/STATE"**. They are looking for a couple of key people to work with. The reason I'm calling you is because they would much rather offer these positions to people who come highly recommended through personal referrals as opposed to running ads in the paper. Newspaper ads don't always bring the top quality candidates that they are looking for. This may or may not be for you, but you might know of someone that would like a chance at a top position in the company that is growing rapidly or someone that would like to supplement their income an extra $1500-$2000 a month part-time.

They have a short DVD that will explain everything. Watch it and let me know what you think. Please keep in mind anyone you know in the area or in other areas around the country that this might apply to. When can I drop this off for you?

NOTE: Get the DVD into their hands immediately. Urgency is very important. Make sure you let them know that they need to watch the DVD tonight or tomorrow morning because you have several people that want to see the DVD.

It's important that you speak with them within 24 hrs. of viewing the DVD. Prompt follow-up is one of the keys to success. Be yourself and be casual. No one likes pushy people. Have fun!!!

Genealogy Report

> ### Script Tip!
> *SMILE WHILE YOU'RE ON THE PHONE. YOU ARE NOT A SALESPERSON, YOU ARE A BUSINESS DEVELOPER.*
>
> *You need to be non-chalant, non-threatening and non-abrasive.*

Hi **"PROSPECT'S NAME"**, how's it going? This is **"YOUR NAME"**. Your name was referred to me as someone who is possibly looking to generate a solid income from home. What can I do for you?

> **INSTRUCTIONS:** *IF they are looking to generate a solid income then go to the Prospecting Script in Dani Johnson's Prospecting and Closing Script Book™.*

> **INSTRUCTIONS:** *IF they are not looking to generate a solid income continue below.*

Ok just to let you know there are thousands of people that are currently being called from **"PROSPECT'S PRIOR BUSINESS"**. We are interviewing for someone who is going to head up an entire organization right there in **"CITY/STATE"**. So if you happen to be looking for or maybe you know somebody that is looking to generate an extra $50,000-$100,000 a year part-time from home I'll go ahead and give you my name and phone number. My name is _____ and phone number is _____.

Can you repeat that back to me? **"PROSPECT'S NAME"** would you by any chance know anybody off hand that would be looking to generate an extra $50,000-$100,000 a year and that would like to head up an entire organization right there in **"CITY/STATE"**?

(If they say "no")
Ok awesome, in the event you run into somebody you've got my name and phone number please pass it on. Thanks so much and God Bless.

(If they say "yes")
Ok awesome.
Do you have a pen and paper handy?
To save us both time, I need to ask you a few questions to figure out what information to direct you to.

(Proceed with the question section of the <u>Prospecting Script</u> in Dani Johnson's Prospecting and Closing Script Book^{TM}.)

Trade Show Script

INSTRUCTIONS: *This is for leads that were collected at a trade show.*

Script Tip!
SMILE WHILE YOU'RE ON THE PHONE. YOU ARE NOT A SALESPERSON, YOU ARE A BUSINESS DEVELOPER.

Hi **"PROSPECT'S NAME"**, how's it going?
This is **"YOUR NAME"** from **"COMPANY NAME"**. We are just doing a quick courtesy call. We met at the **"TRADE SHOW NAME/COMPANY NAME"** the other day.
By the way how did you hear about the **"TRADE SHOW NAME"**?
Did you enjoy it?
So where are you from? What do you do? Etc.
(F.O.R.M. *the prospect)*

Hey **"PROSPECT'S NAME"**, you know you mentioned *(repeat their needs, strengths and goals)*. I work with a company that is expanding all over the country right now. I don't know if you have the skills and the qualities of the kind of person that they're looking for and I'm sure you're totally satisfied with your current job. Why don't we get together and I can get you some information of what they have available. If it's a match great, if not, that's fine too. At least it's a chance for you to *(repeat their needs, strengths and goals)*. So when are you available?

> **INSTRUCTIONS:** *When you follow-up continue to build a rapport and direct them to your website, recorded call, schedule them for a live meeting, etc.*

If the prospect asks "What's it all about?"

That's a really good question; it's about a way for you to be able to *(repeat their needs, strengths and goals)*. And who knows it may or may not work for you, I don't know. But once you get a hold of the information you will be able to see whether or not it's a solid chance to be able to improve *(repeat their needs, strengths and goals)*. So when are you available?

Button/T-Shirt Script

> ### Script Tip!
> *SMILE WHEN YOU ARE APPROACHED! BE YOURSELF AND BE CASUAL. YOU ARE NOT A SALESPERSON, YOU ARE A BUSINESS DEVELOPER.*
>
> *The point of the button/t-shirt is to get the prospect to make contact with you, not to sell them on the spot.*

Prospect: So tell me about your button / t-shirt.

<u>You Say:</u> What's your name? Hi **"PROSPECT'S NAME"**, how's it going?

> ### Script Tip!
> *Put out your hand to shake their hand. F.O.R.M. your prospect. Don't assume you know everything about them. Ask questions.*

> ## Your Next Step...
>
> *Go to the Face to Face Conversation Approach Script in Dani Johnson's Prospecting and Closing Script Book™.*

If the prospect asks what company you are with, say:

I work with a national/international firm who specializes in business development and marketing. What do you do?

> **Script Tip!**
> *Bridge back to controlling the conversation by asking your prospect questions.*

Prospect Cuts You Off With Questions (a.k.a. The "Jerk" Script)

> **Script Tip!**
> *SMILE WHILE YOU'RE ON THE PHONE. YOU ARE NOT A SALESPERSON, YOU ARE A BUSINESS DEVELOPER.*

You know **"PROSPECT'S NAME"**, right now, I'm interviewing for a long-term business relationship and this is not quite getting off on the right foot. So if you are absolutely serious about generating a 6 figure income working from home, I have a few simple questions that I need to ask you in order to direct you to the right information. If you are not serious about developing that 6 figure income working part time from home, then I'll just go ahead and give you my name and phone number and when you get more serious or if you run into someone who is serious, you can give me a call. So are you ready to get the information you requested so you can generate that income from home and *(repeat their needs, strengths and goals)*?

More Dani Johnson

Voice Mail Scripts

Voice Mail To Leave On The Third Try

INSTRUCTIONS: *You are not talking to a machine you are talking to a live person who will be listening to this message. Leave the message as though you are talking to a friend not a stranger. If you are working a lot of leads, call 3 different times a day and leave a message on the third try.*

Script Tip!
SMILE WHILE YOU'RE ON THE PHONE. YOU ARE NOT A SALESPERSON, YOU ARE A BUSINESS DEVELOPER.

Hi **"PROSPECT'S NAME"**. *(like "where are you??")*

This is **"YOUR NAME"**. I've been trying to get a hold of you and this is the third time that I have called. This is the last time that I will be calling you to get you the information that you requested about generating an income working from home. We will be making our decision in the next 48 hours from this advertising campaign so if you're serious give me a call and I'll get that information to you and we'll see if you have the qualities of the kind of person that we're looking for. At that point we'll decide whether or not we'll be able to work together. If you're just curious no need to return the phone call. Again my name is _____ and my phone number is _____. Again, that's **"YOUR NUMBER"**. Have an awesome day and God bless.

Good Prospect Does Not Show Up On The Follow Up Call

INSTRUCTIONS: *You are not talking to a machine you are talking to a live person who will be listening to this message. Leave the message as though you are talking to a friend not a stranger.*

Script Tip!
SMILE WHILE YOU'RE ON THE PHONE. YOU ARE NOT A SALESPERSON, YOU ARE A BUSINESS DEVELOPER.

Hey **"PROSPECT'S NAME"**, this is **"YOUR NAME"**. I hope something didn't happen to you or someone in your family. We had an appointment today at **"TIME OF APPT"**. I know that you're definitely not the kind of person who wouldn't follow through on a commitment you made to make an appointment. I know something must have happened. So why don't you go ahead and give me a call back, I just want to make sure that you're okay and everything is fine. My phone number is _____. Again, that's **"YOUR NUMBER"**.

Hey listen on this appointment we had – don't worry about it. If it doesn't work, that's absolutely fine. I just want to know you're alright.

(If they don't call back – NEXT them!)

55

Genealogy Report Voice Mail

> **INSTRUCTIONS:** *You are not talking to a machine you are talking to a live person who will be listening to this message. Leave the message as though you are talking to a friend not a stranger.*

Script Tip!
SMILE WHILE YOU'RE ON THE PHONE. YOU ARE NOT A SALESPERSON, YOU ARE A BUSINESS DEVELOPER.

Hi **"PROSPECT'S NAME"**, how's it going? This is **"YOUR NAME"**. Your name was referred to me as someone who is possibly looking to generate a solid income from home. Thousands of people are currently being called from your **"PROSPECT'S PRIOR BUSINESS"** and if you are serious about generating an extra $50,000-$100,000 a year working part-time from home then give me a call. My phone number is _____. *(Repeat your phone number a 2nd time)* We are looking for someone that's going to be at the top of this organization and we'll be making our decision real soon from this list. It's a first come first serve basis. So I hope to hear from you in the next 24 hours. Thanks so much and have an awesome day.

More Dani Johnson
Closing Scripts

Spousal Objection

INSTRUCTIONS: *When receiving the objection keep smiling, keep your posture strong, don't weaken and get defensive. This script is used when you have completed the Prospecting Script in Dani Johnson's Prospecting and Closing Script Book™ and you're calling them to see if they have reviewed the information yet.*

Script Tip!
SMILE WHILE YOU'RE ON THE PHONE. YOU ARE NOT A SALESPERSON, YOU ARE A BUSINESS DEVELOPER.

Prospect: I need to talk with my husband/wife.

You Say: Ok **"PROSPECT'S NAME"**. I totally understand and that is important. So **"PROSPECT'S NAME"**, is it that you are absolutely serious about *(repeat their needs, strengths and goals)* and that you run **all** *(pause)* of your decisions by your "husband/wife" first or are you just telling me that you need to talk to your "husband/wife" because you are not serious at **all** about *(repeat their needs, strengths and goals)* and you don't want to hurt my feelings?

(If the prospect's response is...)
Prospect: Actually I don't need to talk to my husband/wife.

You Say: Great! Welcome aboard. How do you want your name spelled on your checks?

(If the prospect's response is...)
Prospect: No I'm serious I just need to talk to my husband/wife.

You Say: Have you ever brought something home to your "husband/wife" that you were excited about?

Did "he/she" end up asking questions you couldn't answer?

Did "he/she" kind of 'poke some holes' in your excitement?

Was that a little frustrating?

Would you say that bypassing frustration would be a good idea?

We have two options. One, we could go ahead and let your "husband/wife" take a look at the information in the same exact way that you did and "he/she" can drill me with questions instead of you. And at that point the two of you can decide whether or not this is something you want to move forward on so that you can *(repeat their needs, strengths and goals)*. Or we can go ahead, get you started right away and start building your check this week and you could just show "him/her" the check. So which will it be **"PROSPECT'S NAME"**, do you want to show "him/her" the check?

Great, welcome aboard!

Pyramid Objection

> **INSTRUCTIONS:** *When receiving the objection keep smiling, keep your posture strong, don't weaken and get defensive. This question simply shows their ignorance.*

> **Script Tip!**
> *SMILE WHILE YOU'RE ON THE PHONE. YOU ARE NOT A SALESPERSON, YOU ARE A BUSINESS DEVELOPER.*

Prospect: Is this a pyramid?

You Say: What do you mean by that?

Prospect: You know when you have to sign your friends and family members up.

You Say: Is that what you are looking for?

Prospect: NO!

You Say: Oh good! We actually work with an advertising firm. We interview people to see if they are qualified to be in a home based business and those that are we establish them in business.

So **"PROSPECT'S NAME"**, do you want to make a little or a lot so that you can *(repeat their needs, strengths and goals)*? Great, welcome aboard! How do you want your name spelled on your checks?

"I Don't Like Sales" Objection

INSTRUCTIONS: *When receiving the objection keep smiling, keep your posture strong, don't weaken and get defensive. This question is just revealing the prospects fear of failure.*

Script Tip!
SMILE WHILE YOU'RE ON THE PHONE. YOU ARE NOT A SALESPERSON, YOU ARE A BUSINESS DEVELOPER.

Prospect: I don't like sales.

You Say: What do you mean by that?

Prospect: You know, where I have to go and sell stuff to my friends and family members.

You Say: Is that what you're looking for?

Prospect: No!

You Say: Great, welcome aboard!

Another Scenario:

Prospect: Is this sales?,

You Say: What do you mean by that?

Prospect: Do I have to be pushy and try to sell my friends on this stuff?

You Say: Is that what you're looking for?

Prospect: No!

You Say: Great, that's not what we want you to do. Welcome aboard! How do you want your name spelled on your checks?

If the prospect is persistent with firing questions away, take control of the conversation and say:

"PROSPECT'S NAME", it sounds like you have some really good questions and concerns.
What's your first question?
What's your second question?
Do you have a third question? *(No more than 3 questions)*

So **"PROSPECT'S NAME"**, if I can answer your questions and you feel really good and satisfied with the answers, are you ready to get started right away so you can *(repeat their needs, strengths and goals)*?

(Answer these questions without selling. Be quick, clear and concise.)

Does that answer your 1st question?
Does that answer your 2nd question? Etc.

(After the last question has been answered then say...)

Great. Welcome aboard! How do you want your name spelled on your checks?

64

"I Don't Have The Time" Objection

> **INSTRUCTIONS:** *When receiving the objection keep smiling, keep your posture strong, don't weaken and get defensive.*

> **Script Tip!**
> *SMILE WHILE YOU'RE ON THE PHONE. YOU ARE NOT A SALESPERSON, YOU ARE A BUSINESS DEVELOPER.*

Prospect: I don't have the time.

You Say: Yeah **"PROSPECT'S NAME"**, I totally understand. So is it that you are really serious about *(repeat their needs, strengths, and goals)* and that you have some concerns about time or are you just telling me you don't have the time because you are not serious at all about *(repeat their needs, strengths and goals)* and you don't want to hurt my feelings?"

Prospect: No, no. I am deadly serious about *(needs, strengths and goals)*. I can't see how I can do that.

You Say: Ok great, it sounds like you have some really good questions and concerns.
What's your first question?

Prospect: How much time is it going to take?

You Say: What's your second question? Do you have a third question? *(No more than 3 questions)*

So **"PROSPECT'S NAME"**, if I can answer your questions and you feel really good and satisfied with the answers, are you ready to get started right away so you can *(repeat their needs, strengths and goals)*?

(Answer these questions without selling. Be quick, clear and concise.)

Does that answer your 1st question?
Does that answer your 2nd question? Etc.

(After the last question has been answered then say...)

Great. Welcome aboard! How do you want your name spelled on your checks?

"I Don't Have The Money" or "I Can't Afford It" Objection

> **INSTRUCTIONS:** *When receiving the objection keep smiling, keep your posture strong, don't weaken and get defensive. 99% of the time the prospect is lying to you about the money. If the prospect's life depended on it they could find the money.*

> ### Script Tip!
> *SMILE WHILE YOU'RE ON THE PHONE. YOU ARE NOT A SALESPERSON, YOU ARE A BUSINESS DEVELOPER.*

So **"PROSPECT'S NAME"**, is it that you are absolutely serious about *(repeat their needs, strengths and goals)* and that you have fallen on some serious hard times and you don't have the extra money or are you just telling me that you can't afford it because you're really not serious at all about *(repeat their needs, strengths and goals)* and you don't want to hurt my feelings?

(If they REALLY don't have the money)

Well **"PROSPECT'S NAME"**, I typically don't do this unless I'm absolutely convinced and certain that the person is deadly serious. If I am certain that we are not going to waste each other's time then I am willing to take a risk on you. I can pre-launch your business if I know that you are serious, in fact as serious as Dani Johnson.

She had $2.03 to her name and a $35,000 debt. She was destitute broke and living out of her car. Not wanting to end up in that financial position again, she found a way to get started and made $2000 profit her first 10 hours from a pay phone booth, $6,500 in 30 hours, and $10,000 the next month.

By the end of her first year, she made a quarter of a million dollars. By the end of her second year, she made her first million. So **"PROSPECT'S NAME"**, are you as serious as she was?

(If the answer is yes)

Tell me why?
Ok great, welcome aboard!
Do you have a pen and paper handy? I have homework for you.

We are going to get your training underway and let's see if we can earn you the money to get yourself started. But **"PROSPECT'S NAME"** if you don't do the homework, I'm sorry, we will have to cut our losses early, okay? So if you do this, I'll know you're serious and I'll take you to the next step.

1. Go to www.danijohnson.com/video that's D-A-N-I Johnson.com forward slash video and watch the video.
2. Click on the 'Home' page and register as a free member. Find and listen to the call dated 8/29/05.
3. Make a list of goals
4. Make a list of resources

"I Need To Wait 2 Weeks For The Money" Objection

> **INSTRUCTIONS:** *When receiving the objection keep smiling, keep your posture strong, don't weaken and get defensive.*

> *Script Tip!*
> *SMILE WHILE YOU'RE ON THE PHONE. YOU ARE NOT A SALESPERSON, YOU ARE A BUSINESS DEVELOPER.*

You Say: Ok **"PROSPECT'S NAME"**, is it that you're serious about *(repeat their needs, strengths and goals)* and you really don't have the money or are you just telling me that you need to wait 2 weeks for the money because you're not serious at all about *(repeat their needs, strengths and goals)* and you don't want to hurt my feelings?

Prospect: No I am absolutely serious about *(needs, strengths and goals)*. I just need to wait for the money to come in.

You Say: Okay, great. Welcome aboard! **"PROSPECT'S NAME"** do you have a pen and paper handy?

Prospect: Yes.

You Say: Great, I have some instructions for you. Let's at least give you a head start. **"PROSPECT'S NAME"** this is how our relationship is going to work. I am going to give you some homework and if you follow through with it then I know how serious you are. At that point I will give you the next step. Are you ready to write this down?

(You are basically getting the person involved. Put them to work even though you haven't received the money yet.)

1. Go to www.danijohnson.com/video that's D-A-N-I Johnson.com forward slash video and watch the video.
2. Click on the 'Home' page and register as a free member. Find and listen to the call dated 8/29/05.
3. Make a list of goals
4. Make a list of resources

Alternate Money Objection Script
When You Know They Have The Money

INSTRUCTIONS: *When receiving the objection keep smiling, keep your posture strong, don't weaken and get defensive.*

Script Tip!
SMILE WHILE YOU'RE ON THE PHONE. YOU ARE NOT A SALESPERSON, YOU ARE A BUSINESS DEVELOPER.

Prospect: I don't have the money right now.

You Say: What do you mean by that?

Prospect: Well, I'm not sure I can come up with all the cash right now...but...well... I guess I could use the VISA.

(Let them talk themselves into it.)

You Say: Great, welcome aboard! How do you want your name spelled on your checks?

"I Haven't Looked At The Information Yet" Objection

INSTRUCTIONS: *When receiving the objection keep smiling, keep your posture strong, don't weaken and get defensive. This script is used when you have completed the Prospecting Script in Dani Johnson's Prospecting and Closing Script Book™ and you're calling them to see if they have reviewed the information yet.*

Script Tip!
SMILE WHILE YOU'RE ON THE PHONE. YOU ARE NOT A SALESPERSON, YOU ARE A BUSINESS DEVELOPER.

You Ask: Did you get a chance to review the information yet?

Prospect: No.

You Say: Really? Did you have some kind of disaster happen in your family?

Prospect: No.

You Say: Oh, okay you know **"PROSPECT'S NAME"** I certainly don't want to waste your time or mine and I typically don't give people a second chance, put if I'm absolutely certain that you are deadly serious about *(repeat their needs, strengths and goals)*, then I will give you a second chance. So you tell me, are you serious about *(repeat their needs, strengths and goals)*?

Prospect: Yes.

You Say: Great! Do you have a pen and paper handy?

Prospect: Yes.

You Say: Do you have access to the internet while you are on the phone with me?

Prospect: Yes.

You Say: Go ahead and go over to the computer now. I want to make sure you have no problems downloading the information.

(While they are heading to the computer get them to talk about what is important to them.)

You Say: Were you able to download the information?

Prospect: Yes.

You Say: Ok, go ahead and review that information right now and I'll call you back in 15 minutes. At that point, we're going to decide whether or not we're going to work together and where you fit in on the team. At least it's a way for you to *(repeat their needs, strengths and goals)*. So I'll call you back in 15 minutes.

(If the prospect is really not serious about their needs, strengths and goals, etc. use the script below.)

Okay **"PROSPECT'S NAME"**, write this down: Here's my phone number. When you get a little more serious about *(repeat their needs, strengths and goals)*, why don't you go ahead and give me a call. Good luck and God bless and I hope you find what you're looking for.

73

"I Did Not Request Information" *and/ or* "I'm Not Interested" Objection

---

> ### Script Tip!
> *SMILE WHILE YOU'RE ON THE PHONE. YOU ARE NOT A SALESPERSON, YOU ARE A BUSINESS DEVELOPER.*
>
> *F.O.R.M. your prospects. Remember you are the interviewer.*

Prospect Says:
"I didn't request information and/or I'm not interested."

You Say:
Gee, I'm sorry I want to make sure that the advertising firm that we're working with is not giving us false informa-tion. So you're **"PROSPECT'S FULL NAME"** in **"CITY/ STATE"**? And I have you at **"PROSPECT'S NUMBER"**? That's strange it shows that you requested information about making money from home. Is that right?

(If the prospect says yes)

Great, do you have a pen and paper handy? To save us both time, I need to ask you a few questions to figure out what information to direct you to.

(If the prospect says no)

Ok **"PROSPECT'S NAME"**, you know what, we happen to be targeting **"CITY"** specifically. We are actually interviewing for someone that's going to head up an entire organization right there in **"CITY/STATE"**. Depending on experience and skills we have a 6 figure position available as well as part-time position for $2,000-$3,000 a month. Would you happen to know anybody that would be looking for a 6-figure position or part-time position for $2,000-$3,000 a month?

"I Joined Another Business" Objection

> ### Script Tip!
> *SMILE WHILE YOU'RE ON THE PHONE. YOU ARE NOT A SALESPERSON, YOU ARE A BUSINESS DEVELOPER.*

Prospect Says:
"I joined another business."

You Say:
Great! Good for you. When did you join?

If it was 1 week or so ago say

Okay, I want to make sure that the advertising firm we are working with is not giving us false information. So you're **"PROSPECT'S FULL NAME"** in **"CITY/STATE"**? And I have you at **"PROSPECT'S NUMBER"**?
That's strange it shows that you requested information just a few days ago about making money from home. Is that right?

(If the prospect says yes)

Great, do you have a pen and paper handy?
To save us both time, I need to ask you a few questions to figure out what information to direct you to.

> ### *Your Next Step...*
>
> *Go straight to F.O.R.M.ing them and proceed with the question section of the **Prospecting Script** in Dani Johnson's Prospecting and Closing Script Book™.*

(If the prospect says no)

Well, hey, why don't I do this, I'll give you my name and phone number, and in the event that you're not going to get the proper skills, training and development to be able to build that 6 figure income over there, we happen to work with a trainer who has a track record of helping people generate 6 figures.

We are actually interviewing for someone who is going to start up an entire organization right there in **"CITY/STATE"**. Depending on experience and skills we have a 6 figure position available as well as part-time position for $2000-$3000 a month.

Do you have a pen and paper handy?
My name is _____ and my phone number is _____."
Give it a 2nd time.
(Then ask the prospect to repeat your phone number)
Have an awesome day and God bless!

> **INSTRUCTIONS:** *Put prospect's name in a follow-up log and call back in a month or so.*

"I Have To Think About It" Objection

INSTRUCTIONS: *When receiving the objection keep smiling, keep your posture strong, don't weaken and get defensive.*

Script Tip!
SMILE WHILE YOU'RE ON THE PHONE. YOU ARE NOT A SALESPERSON, YOU ARE A BUSINESS DEVELOPER.

Prospect: Sounds great but I need to think about it.

You Say: Ok **"PROSPECT'S NAME"**, is it that you're serious about *(repeat their needs, strengths and goals)* and that you really need to think about it because you have unanswered questions and concerns or are you just telling me that you need to think about it because you're not serious at all and you don't want to hurt my feelings?

Prospect: No I am serious about *(needs, strengths and goals)* I just need to think about it.

You Say: **"PROSPECT'S NAME"** it sounds like you have some really good questions and concerns.

What's your first question?
What's your second question?
Do you have a third question? *(No more than 3 questions)*

So **"PROSPECT'S NAME"**, if I can answer your questions and you feel really good and satisfied with the answers, are you ready to get started right away so you can *(repeat their needs, strengths and goals)*?

(Answer these questions without selling. Be quick, clear and concise.)

Does that answer your 1st question?
Does that answer your 2nd question? Etc.

(After the last question has been answered then say...)

Great. Welcome aboard! How do you want your name spelled on your checks?

Alternate Script Involvement Process - "I Have To Think About It" Objection

---

INSTRUCTIONS: *When receiving the objection keep smiling, keep your posture strong, don't weaken and get defensive. This is a non confrontational approach.*

Script Tip!
SMILE WHILE YOU'RE ON THE PHONE. YOU ARE NOT A SALESPERSON, YOU ARE A BUSINESS DEVELOPER.

Prospect: I need to think about it...

You Say: You know what, that's great. I totally agree with you. You really should think about it because this is an important decision. So listen, I've got a great way for you to think about it. That is, of course, if you are a true "think it over" person. We both have collected information from somebody saying we would think about it and the information ended up in the trash.

So **"PROSPECT'S NAME"**, is it that you are serious about *(repeat their needs, strengths and goals)* and that you have some concerns and unanswered questions or are you just telling me that you need to think about it because you are not serious at all about *(repeat their needs, strengths and goals)* and you don't want to hurt my feelings?

Prospect: No I am serious about *(needs, strengths and goals)*.

You Say: Ok great. Do you have a pen and paper handy?

Prospect: Yeah.

Script Tip!
Direct the prospect to Dani Johnson's Monday Night Home Business Success Call or DaniJohnson.com training call vault, etc.

You Say: I am going to direct you to the information about who our trainer is. Write down www.DaniJohnson.com/video that's D-A-N-I Johnson.com forward slash video.

After watching the video click on 'Home' page and register as a free member. Listen to the call dated August 29, 2005. Take a look at it from the prospective of whether or not you can do something like this. The other thing that we suggest is that you get our 'think it over kit' as well as try our "product/service" risk free and at that point you can see if this is something you can get behind. Go ahead and fill this out so we can get you on your way to your research.

INSTRUCTIONS: *Get them on your LIVE company call. Invite them to a LIVE Training or LIVE Business Presentation.*

Schedule them homework. Just get them to show up for something. The more they come to 'hang out' without pressure, many of them will eventually join.

Follow Up Call #1 *and* They Did Not Do Their Homework

INSTRUCTIONS: *When receiving the objection keep smiling, keep your posture strong, don't weaken and get defensive. After you have signed them up and this appointment is for the next day to go over their homework assignment with them.*

Script Tip!
SMILE WHILE YOU'RE ON THE PHONE. YOU ARE NOT A SALESPERSON, YOU ARE A BUSINESS DEVELOPER.

Hey **"PROSPECT'S NAME"**, did you get a chance to do that homework assignment?

(If the prospect says no)

Did something bad happen to your family?

(If they say "No, I just got too busy and some things just came up.")

Oh, okay well you know **"PROSPECT'S NAME"** I don't want to waste your time and I certainly don't want to waste mine. Our advertising campaign has been extremely successful.

In fact I have a couple appointments to get to. When we spoke yesterday you said you were deadly serious about *(repeat their needs, strengths and goals)*. Were you just playing around when you told me that or were you deadly serious about it? *(Let them respond)*

We certainly didn't help you to get established in business for you to fail. We agreed to start you because I thought you were serious about succeeding. Is that still true?

Well **"PROSPECT'S NAME"**, I am going to give you a second chance to complete the assignment. Do you have access to the internet while talking to me?

(If the prospect says yes)

Go to www.DaniJohnson.com, that's D-A-N-I Johnson.com, and listen to the August 29, 2005 call. I am going to give you an hour and a half to complete the homework assignment. Okay?

Great, I'll call you back in an hour and a half.
(Or you can tell them to call you back)

The 2nd & 3rd Exposure Script

INSTRUCTIONS: *Use this script if you have multiple exposure in the form of: calls, DVDs, websites, etc. that the prospect needs to review before they make a decision. No matter what the prospect says use the following script to introduce what they saw or heard.*

Script Tip!
SMILE WHILE YOU'RE ON THE PHONE. YOU ARE NOT A SALESPERSON, YOU ARE A BUSINESS DEVELOPER.

Hi **"PROSPECT'S NAME"**, how's it going? This is **"YOUR NAME"**. Before you figure out whether or not this is for you maybe you should look over the rest of the information. I would rather you make a good solid decision rather than a hasty one. Have you ever jumped into something with both feet and regretted it? Or have you ever not jumped into something and wished you had? The company has put together two additional *(calls, DVDs, website, etc.)* that will help you make a good solid decision either to do it or not to do it.

I just want you to be sure that in a year from now when someone comes to you and tells you about **"COMPANY NAME"** that you will either say "I'm already in and I'm doing well" or "You know what I checked that out and it really wasn't for me."

So **"PROSPECT'S NAME"**, keep in mind as you're reviewing the information, of anyone you know who needs our **"PRODUCT/SERVICE"** or would like to take advantage of the top positions in the company nationwide. This may or may not work out for you, but who knows it might be a way for you to *(repeat their needs, strengths and goals)*. All I know is the company is moving very fast.

INSTRUCTIONS: *Remember to schedule a time to talk to them immediately after they have reviewed the information. Follow-up is the key to success!!!*

Appendix A

Words *NOT* To Use

Sell
Get involved
In the business
Marketing plan
Levels
Recruit
I
Downline / Upline Under Me
Meeting
Would you be interested?
Are you making what you're worth?
Opportunity of a lifetime
Network Marketing
Multi-Level Marketing

When dealing with nutritional products
Pills
Lose Weight

Words *TO* Use

Move product, market
Get Started
With our company
Profit Plan
Positions
Enroll
We
My / Your team, Sales force, Marketing team
Company overview
Would you be willing to take a look
Are you at least willing
Are you doing what you want to do
I don't want you to miss out on a chance for you to (goals)
We represent an international marketing team
I work with a group of entrepreneurs

When dealing with nutritional products
Tablets
Weight Management

Appendix B

DaniJohnson.com Contact Sheet

Name	Phone	Email	Comments

	Appt	Follow Up	Comments

Appendix C

List Your Goals:

Appendix D

More DaniJohnson.com Resources To Help You Succeed!

If you've benefited from this Prospecting and Closing Script Book™ and accompanying training audios, then you'll find the following resources will help you even more.

Become a FREE www.WorkAtHomeProfitZone.com member – Access over 30 hours of training calls recorded live with Dani Johnson 100% FREE for you and your team. Register now!

FREE weekly training calls for you and your group with Dani Johnson every Monday night @ 7pm PST (10pm EST) Call 512-225-9400, pin 953953#.

Prospect & Close Your Way To Millions Home Study Course!
Who Else Wants to Learn How to Bring Tough Prospects to Their Knees as You Effortlessly Handle Their Objections and Watch Them Talk Themselves Right Into Joining Your Program?
Get the Live DVD's and audios from one of Dani's Prospect & Close Your Way To Millions training seminars!
Visit: DaniJohnson.com/product

Dani Johnson Live - Foundational Tools Essential To 6-Figure Success In Your Home Business on CD!
FINALLY... Training CD's Guaranteed To Turn You Into An MLM, Network Marketing or Home Business Pro!
Get the audios from one of Dani's entire Live 2 Day Seminar on 10 CD's! Visit: DaniJohnson.com/product

1 on 1 Coaching!

If you would like to receive personal 1 on 1 training and coaching from Dani to help you master prospecting and closing using these scripts or coach you on ANY other aspect of building your business successfully, contact us at DaniJohnson.com/support or call 866-760-8255 for rates and more information.

Training Calls for your team or company!

To have Dani do a special Training Call for your team or company, contact us at DaniJohnson.com/support or call 866-760-8255 for rates and more information.

Attend a Live 2 Day Seminar with Dani!

Discover what's been holding YOU back and learn the EXACT tools that took this young woman from living out of her car... to making her FIRST MILLION in under 2 years! Visit: DaniJohnson.com/seminar for more information and to register for the next live seminar!

Attend a Live 3 Day Advanced Seminar!

Do you want to be equipped to develop a powerful sales force filled with top producing independent leaders?
Once you attend a Live 2 Day Seminar with Dani then you will qualify for the Live 3 Day Advanced Seminar, Creating A Dynasty. For the elite who have attended both Live Seminars you may be chosen, upon meeting qualifications, for the DaniJohnson.com Mentoring Program. Visit: DaniJohnson.com/seminar for more information and to register for the next live seminar!

We want to hear from you! Please send your comments or testimonials to DaniJohnson.com/support. Thanks and God bless!

Notes: